My Muslim Year

Cath Senker

HODDER
Wayland

an imprint of Hodder Children's Books

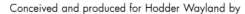
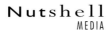

Titles in this series
My Buddhist Year • My Christian Year • My Hindu Year
My Jewish Year • My Muslim Year • My Sikh Year

Conceived and produced for Hodder Wayland by

Nutshell
MEDIA

Intergen House, 65-67 Western Road, Hove, BN3 2JQ, UK
www.nutshellmedialtd.co.uk

Editor: Polly Goodman
Inside designer and illustrator: Peta Morey
Cover designer: Tim Mayer
Consultant: Shahrukh Husain

Published in Great Britain in 2003 by Hodder Wayland, an imprint of Hodder Children's Books.

British Library Cataloguing in Publication Data
Senker, Cath
My Muslim year. - (A year of religious festivals)
1. Fasts and feasts - Islam - Juvenile literature
I. Title
297.3'6

ISBN 0 7502 4052 0

Printed in Hong Kong by Wing King Tong.

Hodder Children's Books
A division of Hodder Headline Limited
338 Euston Road, London NW1 3BH

Acknowledgements: The author would like to thank Nayaab and Yasmin Sattar, and Amanda Hill, Head of RE at West Hove Junior School, Sussex, for all their help in the preparation of this book.

Picture Acknowledgements:
Britstock 4, 11, 13, 22, 25 (Peter Sanders); Eye Ubiquitous 6 (Julia Waterlow), 9 (John Hulme), 14 (James Davis Worldwide); Hodder Wayland Picture Library 18 (Julia Waterlow); Impact 15 (Caroline Penn); Nutshell Media 2 (Yiorgo Nikiteas); Peter Sanders Cover, 7, 8, 10, 12, 14, 24; World Religions Title page, 16, 19, 20, 21, 23, 26, 27 (Christine Osborne).

Cover photograph: Children in Kenya celebrating Milad an-Nabi.
Title page: Children dressed up for Id ul-Adha, in Cairo.

Contents

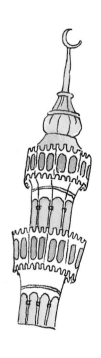

Note: When Muslims say the name of one of the prophets, they always say 'Peace Be Upon Him' afterwards, which is shown in this book as ﷺ.

A Muslim life

Muslims believe in one God, Allah. To Muslims, Islam means accepting the will of God. The holy book, the Qur'an, guides Muslims in their lives.

Muslims pray to Allah five times a day. They give money to help poor people. Muslims fast during the month of Ramadan. Once in their lives they try to go on a pilgrimage.

The Qur'an tells Muslims which foods they should and shouldn't eat.

This is Nayaab with Honey, her rabbit. Nayaab has written a diary about the Muslim festivals.

Nayaab's diary
Sunday 23 February

My name's Nayaab [say 'Nee-yarb'] Sattar. I'm nine years old. I live with my mum, dad, and sister Layla, who's five. I've got a pet rabbit, called Honey. My favourite hobbies are sports, reading and art. We're Muslims and we mostly pray at home. We've got two copies of the Qur'an, plus one on a CD. My favourite festival is Id ul-Fitr.

There are two main Muslim festivals, Id ul-Fitr and Id ul-Adha, and several other special occasions.

The Muslim symbol is the star and crescent.

Fridays

Every Friday

Friday prayers are special. Muslim men stop what they are doing and join other Muslims at the mosque.

Saying prayers together helps people to feel part of the Muslim community – called the 'ummah'.

There are Muslims living all over the world. These men are saying Friday prayers at a mosque in Lanzhou, China.

Girls learn to pray at home with their mother.

At the mosque, Muslims say the midday prayers. Then their imam, or teacher, gives a talk about a part of the Qur'an. He may talk about something that interests Muslims today. Muslim women usually pray at home.

Nayaab's diary
Saturday 1 March

Today I went to religion school at the mosque. Normally I pray at home with my mum, but once a week I go to the mosque for classes. I go with my sister, Layla, and my Muslim friends. Today we read the Qur'an and said one of the five daily prayers together. Going to the mosque is very special to me. It makes me feel closer to Allah.

Hijrah

At Hijrah, Muslims celebrate the start of the Islamic calendar. It began in 622 CE, when the Prophet Muhammad ﷺ and his followers fled to Madinah.

'Hijrah' means migration. Muhammad ﷺ was welcomed in Madinah. He set up an Islamic community.

The Prophet's mosque in Madinah, Saudi Arabia. After Hijrah, Muhammad ﷺ became the leader of Madinah.

Muslims read about the life of the Prophet ﷺ in the Qur'an. The Qur'an is written in Arabic.

At Hijrah, Muslims make a fresh start. They try to 'migrate' from any bad things they did in the past. They move on to a new year, when they will try to do things better.

Nayaab's diary

Wednesday 5 March

Today was Hijrah, the start of the new year. The first month in the Muslim calendar is called Muharram. At Hijrah, Muslims think about how to bring their lives closer to Islam. I thought about the difficult life the Prophet ﷺ led because of his belief in Islam. Grandad went to the mosque to say special prayers and read the Qur'an. It was a quiet, religious day.

9

Ashura

Ashura is a very important festival for Shi'a Muslims. They remember the day when seventeen members of the Prophet's ﷺ family were cruelly killed. Hussain ﷺ, the Prophet's ﷺ grandson, was one of them.

Ashura is on the tenth day of Muharram, the first month of the Muslim year. For nine days beforehand there are religious gatherings.

A procession to mark Ashura in Iran. The men are carrying models of the tombs of Hussain ﷺ and members of his family who died.

These children in Iran are acting out the story of the battle in which Hussain ؊ was killed.

In Shi'a areas, cities close down on Ashura and people join processions to the mosque. They fast, wear black clothes and show their great sorrow. It is a very holy day.

Nayaab's diary
Saturday 15 March

Yesterday it was Ashura. Grandad went to the mosque to pray. My Shi'a friend Yasmin and her family fasted. On Ashura, we remember the grandchildren of the Prophet Muhammad ؊ and how they suffered in the Battle of Karbala. In the end, nearly the whole of the Prophet's ؊ family was wiped out. To remember them, some people give money to a charity especially for children.

Milad an-Nabi

At Milad an-Nabi, Muslims remember the birth and life of the Prophet Muhammad ﷺ. They thank Allah for giving them the Prophet ﷺ. He is an example to them all.

Many Muslims get together in mosques, Muslim centres and houses. The places are decorated with lights and flags.

Children on Lamu Island, Kenya, taking part in the Milad an-Nabi procession.

These two Kenyan girls are reading the Qur'an as part of a competition on Milad an-Nabi.

Everyone is welcome to come to the gatherings. People read about the life of Muhammad ﷺ and chant to praise him. They enjoy a delicious feast.

Nayaab's diary
Wednesday 14 May

Today was Milad an-Nabi. It's not really a celebration because it was the day that Muhammad ﷺ died as well as his birthday. So Milad an-Nabi is a happy day and a sad day at the same time. At the mosque we heard a story about the life of the Prophet ﷺ. We talked about how we should be honest and truthful like him. When we said our daily prayers we added special prayers to remember the Prophet ﷺ.

Lailat ul-Miraj

This festival celebrates the Night of the Ascent. It was when the Prophet Muhammad ﷺ rose up to heaven.

Muhammad ﷺ travelled up through the seven heavens to Allah. On the way, he met all the other prophets, including Moses ﷺ and Abraham ﷺ.

The Dome of the Rock mosque in Jerusalem. It is said that Muhammad ﷺ rose up to heaven from a rock that is inside the mosque.

These girls in Bradford, Britain, have learnt to pray five times a day.

In heaven, Allah told Muhammad ﷺ that Muslims should pray to him more than a hundred times each day. But Muhammad ﷺ said people wouldn't manage that. So they agreed that Muslims should pray five times a day.

Nayaab's diary

Wednesday 24 September

Last night was Lailat ul-Miraj. At the mosque, we practised saying a few prayers. We learnt about the meaning of the night journey of Muhammad ﷺ. My grandad stayed up all night praying. I went home and thought about Muhammad's ﷺ exciting journey and how he travelled up to Allah on a horse. I lay awake in bed waiting for the special moment when people's prayers are granted.

15

Lailat ul-Barat

On this night, Allah decides what will happen to everyone over the next year.

Muslims think about things they have done wrong. They hope that Allah will forgive them for their bad actions. He will reward them for good things they have done.

These Muslims are sharing bread with poor people at a mosque in Pakistan.

These children have been sent clothes and toys by a Muslim charity.

Nayaab's diary
Monday 13 October

Last night was Lailat ul-Barat. I thought about the good and bad things I've done this year. I've given some of my pocket money to a charity for poor children in Pakistan. And I've helped mum with the cleaning. I haven't done anything really bad, but sometimes I've fought with Layla over the computer. I prayed to Allah to forgive me. I feel Allah is watching me all the time and hears my prayers.

Muslims gather to read the Qur'an and to pray all night. They share food with poor people. Muslims believe you must earn forgiveness by doing good things.

Ramadan

Ramadan is the month when Muslims fast. Fasting is one of the important duties of a Muslim.

During daylight hours, all healthy Muslims over 12 years old should go without food and drink. Nothing may pass their lips – not even chewing gum. People must make sure they have only good thoughts and behave well.

Celebrating the end of the fast in China. Muslims often invite guests to break the fast with them.

Here in Cairo, Egypt, Muslims make sure that everyone who has fasted gets enough to eat.

Fasting gives Muslims a wonderful sense of community. They know that all over the world, Muslims are fasting together.

Nayaab's diary
Monday 17 November

Today is the fifth day of Ramadan. This year, for the first time, I've fasted for a few days. I'm not used to it so I got quite hungry. But I felt pleased with myself for managing it! It was really exciting getting up in the night to eat before dawn. Fasting makes me feel I can do anything if I put my mind to it.

Lailat ul-Qadr

Lailat ul-Qadr is the Night of Power. It celebrates the first night that the Qur'an was revealed to the Prophet Muhammad ﷺ. The angel Gabriel appeared and told him to read Allah's message.

These men are saying the dawn prayers in Cairo, Egypt. They have stayed up all night on Lailat ul-Qadr.

The night of Lailat ul-Qadr is during the last ten days of Ramadan. Many people stay up the whole night saying Ramadan prayers.

People also read the Qur'an through the night. Muslims believe they receive special blessings on Lailat ul-Qadr.

Reading the Qur'an is a very important part of all Muslim festivals.

Nayaab's diary
Sunday 23 November

On Friday night it was Lailat ul-Qadr. Grandad and Grandma stayed up quite late and prayed at home. I think the Prophet Muhammad ﷺ was very surprised when the angel Gabriel appeared. Muhammad ﷺ was amazed when the words actually started to come out of his mouth! He must have been excited to be chosen as Allah's messenger.

Id ul-Fitr

Id ul-Fitr is a happy festival that marks the end of Ramadan.

Everyone gets excited when the new moon is seen. It means Ramadan will end the following morning. Muslims hug and wish each other 'Id Mubarak' – 'Happy Id'.

This girl and her mother are looking at the cards people have sent them to wish their family a happy Id.

On Id day, people put on their best clothes. They go to the mosque for special Id prayers. Then families and friends gather for a big lunch and children are given presents.

Muslims give money to make sure that everyone in the community can afford to celebrate Id.

Nayaab's diary
Thursday 27 November

Yesterday was Id ul-Fitr – my favourite festival! I had the day off school and wore my lovely new clothes. I got wonderful presents – jewellery, clay, paints and sandals. We went to my grandma's house for dinner. I love it when all my family gathers together. When I went back to school I brought in chocolates and told people about our festival.

Hajj

During the twelfth Islamic month, Muslims go on Hajj. The word Hajj means pilgrimage, a religious journey.

It is the duty of all Muslims to go on Hajj once in their life. The pilgrims visit the city of Makkah and other holy places in Saudi Arabia.

Pilgrims wear simple white clothes for the whole time that they are on Hajj.

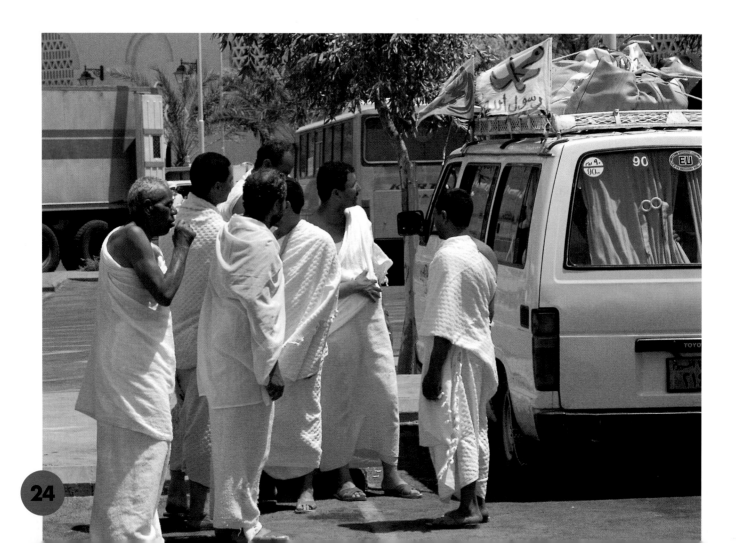

The large black stone in the middle of this mosque is the Ka'aba. It is holy to Muslims.

Nayaab's diary
Sunday 1 February

Hajj was in January this year. My grandparents were lucky enough to go. When they came back, all their friends and family came to say 'congratulations'. They brought back zamzam water, which is holy water for people to drink. Grandad bought an alarm clock in the shape of a mosque. You set it to give the call to prayer at the right times. They had a wonderful time and didn't want to come back.

When the pilgrims are close to Makkah, they change into Hajj clothes, called ihram. They perform special rituals. The rituals celebrate events in the lives of the prophets Abraham ﷺ, Isma'il ﷺ and Muhammad ﷺ.

Id ul-Adha

Id ul-Adha is the biggest Muslim festival. Muslims remember when Allah ordered the Prophet Abraham ﷺ to sacrifice his son. This was to test his faith.

Abraham ﷺ prepared to kill his son, but Allah did not make him do it.

These girls in Cairo, Egypt, have put on their favourite clothes for Id ul-Adha. Everyone likes to look their best for Id.

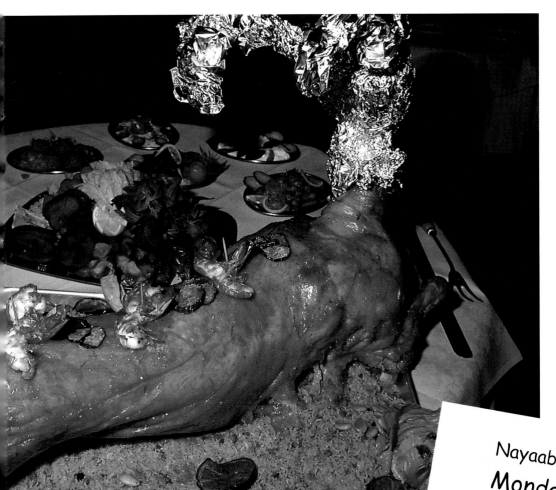

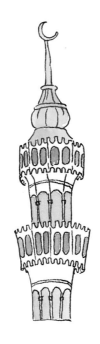

Muslims eat meat at Id ul-Adha.

To celebrate the faith of Abraham ﷺ, people visit the mosque for special prayers. They hold a huge feast with meat. The meat is shared with the whole community. Children are given money, just like on Id ul-Fitr.

Nayaab's diary
Monday 2 February

Today was Id ul-Adha. We said special prayers at home. We talked about how Abraham ﷺ was prepared to sacrifice his son for the love and trust of Allah. To remember this, we ate barbecued lamb for dinner. You're supposed to eat some meat and give the rest away. We sent money to Pakistan to pay for meat to be given to poor people there.

Festival calendar

MUHARRAM

Hijrah (1st day)
Celebrates the move of the Prophet Muhammad ﷺ and his followers to Madinah.

Ashura (1st–10th days)
Muslims remember the death of Hussain ﷺ, the grandson of the Prophet Muhammad ﷺ. The tenth day is the most important.

SAFAR

RABI' AL-AWWAL

Milad an-Nabi (12–17th days)
The birthday of the Prophet Muhammad ﷺ. Celebrations throughout the month.

RABI' AL-THANI

JUMADA AL-AWWAL

JUMADA AL-THANI

Yawm al-Zahrah (20th day)
Birthday of Fatimah Zahrah, daughter of the Prophet Muhammad ﷺ. It is Women's Day in Iran.

RAJAB

Lailat ul-Miraj (27th day)
Celebrates Muhammad ﷺ rising to heaven. Allah told him Muslims should pray five times a day.

SHA'BAN

Lailat ul-Barat (14–15th day)
The Night of Forgiveness, when people's sins are forgiven.

RAMADAN

Ramadan (1st–29th or 30th days)
The month of fasting.

Lailat ul-Qadr (27th day)
The night when Allah revealed the first part of the Qur'an to Muhammad ﷺ. One day, but often remembered over the last ten days of Ramadan.

SHAWAL

Id ul-Fitr (1st day)
The festival to mark the end of the Ramadan fast. Three days' holiday in Muslim countries.

DHUL QAD'AH

DHUL HIJJAH

Hajj (between 8th and 13th days)
The pilgrimage to Makkah and other holy places.

Id ul-Adha (10–12th days)
A feast is held to remember the faith of Abraham ﷺ. Four days' holiday in Muslim countries.

Glossary

Allah God.

ascent Rise. Muhammad ﷺ ascended, or rose, to heaven.

blessings God's help and protection.

fast To go without food and water for religious reasons.

Hajj The religious journey to Makkah that all Muslims try to make once in their lives.

holy Connected with God.

Id A religious holiday for thanking Allah. It is a happy celebration.

ihram The clothes worn by pilgrims. Men wear one sheet of white cloth round the waist and another over the left shoulder. Women wear a long-sleeved robe down to their ankles.

imam Means 'teacher'. A religious leader in Islam.

Islamic To do with Islam, the Muslim religion.

Makkah The city in Arabia where Muhammad ﷺ was born and started to teach his message. He had many enemies there and had to leave.

migration Moving to a new place.

mosque The place where Muslims meet, pray and study.

pilgrim A person who goes to a holy place for religious reasons.

pilgrimage A journey to a holy place for religious reasons.

praise To give thanks and show your respect.

Qur'an The Muslims' holy book, written in Arabic. It contains the word of God, as given to the Prophet Muhammad ﷺ.

revealed Made known to somebody.

rituals Actions that are always done in the same way, as part of a religious ceremony.

sacrifice To make an offering to Allah.

Shi'a Muslims Shi'a Muslims are the second-biggest group of Muslims after Sunni Muslims. They use the same Qur'an and share most of the same beliefs as the Sunnis. There are a few important differences in their beliefs.

ummah The family of Islam all over the world.

zamzam A special well by the mosque in Makkah. Pilgrims collect water from it to drink and take home.

Notes for teachers

pp4–5 Muslims believe there were many prophets who brought Allah's message to the world. Muhammad ﷺ was the last one and is seen as the perfect prophet. Allah revealed his word to Muhammad ﷺ in beautiful Arabic poetry. Muhammad ﷺ taught Allah's message to his followers. He couldn't write, but the words were written down by his close companions. These writings formed the Qur'an, which is always read in Arabic for prayer. The Qur'an guides Muslims in their lives. The book is treated with great respect; it is kept clean and covered.

pp6–7 On Fridays, Muslims leave work to attend midday prayers at the mosque and return afterwards. In Muslim countries, businesses shut for the midday hour on Fridays. The prayers recited are the same as those said at home on other days. Muslims learn to say them in Arabic. They also say their own personal prayers, called du'a, in their daily language. Women don't usually go to the mosque but girls, like Nayaab, may attend religion classes there.

pp8–9 The Prophet Muhammad ﷺ was born in 570 CE and grew up in Makkah, Saudi Arabia. He was a wise man who believed that all people were equal. Muhammad ﷺ fought against corruption and helped the poor. He believed in one god, Allah, and did not worship idols. The rulers of Makkah turned against him, so he and his followers migrated to Madinah. Muhammad ﷺ ruled Madinah fairly and soon many other places accepted Islamic rule.

pp10–11 After Muhammad ﷺ died, his companion Abu Bakr was chosen by some Muslims to be Khalifah – leader of the community. Some Muslims wanted to choose their leaders; they became known as Sunni Muslims. Others, who became known as Shi'a Muslims, believed that their leaders should be from the family of the Prophet ﷺ. Hussain ﷺ, a grandson of Muhammad ﷺ, was killed along with nearly all of the remaining members of the Prophet's ﷺ family by a later Khalifah called Yazid because Hussain ﷺ would not accept him as leader. On Ashura Shi'a Muslims show their grief over the death of Hussain ﷺ through processions and plays enacting the killing.

pp12–13 No one knows the exact date Muhammad ﷺ was born; there are special prayers and gatherings throughout the month of Rabi' al-Awwal. In many South Asian countries, there are large-scale celebrations. People read from the Sira, the biography of Muhammad ﷺ, and recite salutations and songs in his praise. Religious leaders make speeches about his life. Muslims give generously to charity and food is served to guests and the poor. Not all Muslim groups celebrate Milad an-Nabi, for example, Wahabi and Ahmedia Muslims do not celebrate it.

pp14–15 One night the Prophet Muhammad ﷺ was taken by the Angel Jibril (Gabriel) from Makkah to Jerusalem. He travelled up through the seven heavens to Allah, where he led prayers with Ibraham (Abraham) ﷺ , Musa (Moses) ﷺ and other prophets. Islam considers the Jewish prophets, including Jesus ﷺ, to be Islamic prophets too.

pp16–17 On this night, it is believed that Allah decides what people will do over the coming year, who will be born and who will die. During communal prayer, the Arabic formula for repentance 'astaghfirullah' is repeated. People try to stay up all night thanking Allah for their home and family and asking for his blessings. They share food by giving it directly to needy people in the community, or by giving food or money through a mosque or religious organization.

pp18–19 During Ramadan the Qur'an was revealed to the Prophet Muhammad ﷺ. The aim of fasting is to develop self-control; as well as not eating or drinking, Muslims refrain from sex. People should commit no bad deeds such as cheating, gossiping, lying or stealing. The experience helps people to gain spiritual strength, and develop empathy for the poor who go hungry. Giving to charity is vital during Ramadan. The fast is broken at sunset; people eat a couple of dates, then they pray, and later they enjoy a full meal.

pp20–21 People are not sure exactly which day the Qur'an was revealed, so some Muslims go to the mosque to pray every night for the last ten nights of Ramadan. On Lailat ul-Qadr, it is believed that Allah releases the angels from their duties and they come down to Earth with special blessings for the true worshippers of Allah. It is the holiest night of the Muslim year.

pp22–23 Id ul-Fitr and Id ul-Adha (also spelt Eid ul-Fitr and Eid ul-Adha) are the main Islamic religious festivals. Id ul-Fitr is announced when the new moon is sighted; many Muslims listen for the announcement on the radio or TV. The following day, Muslims in non-Muslim countries will take the day off. In Muslim countries there is a three-day holiday. Id is a time for gathering with family and friends. Dried fruit such as dates, and sweets made from nuts and sweetened milk, are eaten. There is no dancing or alcohol at Muslim festivals.

pp24–25 Muslims are expected to perform the Hajj only after they have fulfilled all other Islamic duties, including the education of their children and the marriage of their daughters, and only if they can afford it. There are various rituals performed on Hajj, such as circling the sacred building, the Ka'aba, seven times. All pilgrims change into simple white garments for Hajj, so that from whichever country or social class they come from, they appear equal before Allah. Hajj is a wonderful unifying experience.

pp26–27 The major festival of Islam, Id ul-Adha, is celebrated by people on Hajj and those at home. To commemorate the willingness of Abraham ﷺ to sacrifice his own son to Allah, Muslims sacrifice a sheep, goat or camel for the festival. It represents their own willingness to sacrifice all personal wants and needs in the service of Allah. The animal is killed humanely and a generous share offered to poor Muslims. In Muslim countries, there is a four-day holiday.

p28 The Muslim calendar has twelve lunar months, which means the year is an average of 354 days long. So the Islamic calendar goes backwards through the solar year by about eleven days a year.

Other resources

Artefacts
Articles of Faith, Resource House, Kay Street, Bury, Lancashire BL9 6BU. Tel. 0161 763 6232.
Religion in Evidence, 28b Nunnbrook Road Industrial Estate, Huthwaite, Notts NG17 2HU. Tel. 0800 318686.

Books to read
Celebrate: Id ul-Fitr by Mike Hirst
(Hodder Wayland, 1999)
Celebration Stories: A Present for Salima – A Story About Id ul-Fitr by Kerena Marchant (Hodder Wayland, 2002)
Discovering Religions: Islam by Sue Penney
(Heinemann, 2000)
How I Celebrate by Pam Robson
(Hodder Wayland, 2000)
Keystones: Muslim Mosque by Umar Hegedus and Jak Kilby (A&C Black, 2000)
Muslim Festival Tales by Kerena Marchant
(Hodder Wayland, 2000)
My Belief: I am a Muslim by M. Aggarwal
(Franklin Watts, 2001)
My Life, My Religion: Muslim Imam by Akbar Dad Khan
(Franklin Watts, 2001)
Places of Worship: Mosques by E. Huda Bladon
(Heinemann, 1999)
Sacred Texts: The Qur'an and Islam by Anita Ganeri, Alan Brown & Vivien Cato (Evans, 2002)
Storyteller: Islamic Stories by Anita Ganeri (Evans, 1999)
Where we Worship: Muslim Mosque by Angela Wood
(Franklin Watts, 1998)
World of Festivals: Ramadan and Id ul-Fitr by Rosalind Kerven (Evans, 1999)
World Religions: Islam by R. Tames
(Franklin Watts, 1999)

Photopacks
Living Religions: Islam posterpack and booklet by Thomas Nelson and Sons.
Muslims photopack, by the Westhill Project, available from Adrian Leech, Westhill RE Centre, Tel. 0121 415 2258. E-mail: a.leech@bham.ac.uk

Websites
www.frenchwood.co.uk/islam.htm Muslim primary school children explain their religion.
www.soundvision.com Information about Islam and products for children.
www.theresite.org.uk Includes curriculum resources and IT in RE pages with details of CD-Roms, software and videos, and TV and radio programmes.
www.underfives.co.uk/events.html Lists the dates of main festivals for all major religions.

Index